THE AMERICAN JOURNEY
THE INDIAN-AMERICAN
JOURNEY

by Emma Carlson Berne

pogo

Ideas for Parents and Teachers

Pogo Books let children practice reading informational text while introducing them to nonfiction features such as headings, labels, sidebars, maps, and diagrams, as well as a table of contents, glossary, and index.

Carefully leveled text with a strong photo match offers early fluent readers the support they need to succeed.

Before Reading

- "Walk" through the book and point out the various nonfiction features. Ask the student what purpose each feature serves.
- Look at the glossary together. Read and discuss the words.

Read the Book

- Have the child read the book independently.
- Invite him or her to list questions that arise from reading.

After Reading

- Discuss the child's questions. Talk about how he or she might find answers to those questions.
- Prompt the child to think more. Ask: Do you know any Indian Americans? How are their cultural traditions similar to or different from yours?

Pogo Books are published by Jump!
5357 Penn Avenue South
Minneapolis, MN 55419
www.jumplibrary.com

Copyright © 2020 Jump!
International copyright reserved in all countries. No part of this book may be reproduced in any form without written permission from the publisher.

Library of Congress Cataloging-in-Publication Data

Names: Berne, Emma Carlson, author.
Title: The Indian-American journey / by Emma Carlson Berne.
Description: Minneapolis, MN: Jump!, [2020]
Series: The American Journey
Audience: Ages 7-10.
Includes bibliographical references and index.
Identifiers: LCCN 2018057829 (print)
LCCN 2019002522 (ebook)
ISBN 9781641289214 (ebook)
ISBN 9781641289009 (hardcover : alk. paper)
ISBN 9781641289030 (pbk.)
Subjects: LCSH: East Indian Americans–Juvenile literature.
East Indians–United States–Juvenile literature.
United States–Emigration and immigration–Juvenile literature.
India–Emigration and immigration–Juvenile literature.
Classification: LCC E184.E2 (ebook)
LCC E184.E2 B47 2020 (print) | DDC 305.89/1411073–dc23
LC record available at https://lccn.loc.gov/2018057829

Editor: Susanne Bushman
Designer: Molly Ballanger
Cultural Advisor: Shona Ramchandani

Photo Credits: NOWAK LUKASZ/Shutterstock, cover (tl); Vlad G/Shutterstock, cover (tr); Pixfiction/Shutterstock, cover (bl), cover (br); Dragon Images/Shutterstock, 1; StockImageFactory.com/Shutterstock, 3, 6-7; Dzerkach Viktar/Shutterstock, 4; Zvonimir Atletic/Shutterstock, 5; CRS PHOTO/Shutterstock, 8-9; Africa Studio/Shutterstock, 10 (flag); Arvind Balaraman/Shutterstock, 10 (passport); wong yu liang/Shutterstock, 11; Weekend Images Inc./iStock, 12-13; Alex Wong/Getty, 14-15; FatCamera/iStock, 16; allindiaimages/SuperStock, 17; StanislavBeloglazov/Shutterstock, 18-19; Asia Images Group/Shutterstock, 20-21; MicroStockHub/iStock, 23.

Printed in the United States of America at Corporate Graphics in North Mankato, Minnesota.

TABLE OF CONTENTS

CHAPTER 1

LIFE IN INDIA

India is in South Asia. Many languages are spoken here. Hindi is the most common. The **climate** is tropical. See the Himalayas? Parts of these mountains have snow at the top!

Himalayas

Cities in India are crowded. About 17 percent of the people on Earth live here! Some live in villages. They grow **crops** like rice and wheat.

Hinduism is the most common religion in India. It has many gods. Hindus pray at **temples**. Some pray at home. Others here are Muslim. Some are Buddhists or Christians.

Education is very important in India. Why? It can be hard to get a good job without it. People in India can make a good living. But some do not.

Indian people who can afford to might visit the United States. Why? They see family. They go to U.S. colleges. To do this, they need **visas**.

WHAT DO YOU THINK?

Many Indian people know more than one language. They often learn English in school. Would you like to know more than one language?

नमस्ते

Hello!

CHAPTER 2

COMING TO A NEW LAND

A U.S. law passed in 1965. It helped those with skills **immigrate** here. Having a good education helped, too. It also helped them to have family in America.

पासपोर्ट
PASSPORT

सत्यमेव जयते

भारत गणराज्य
REPUBLIC OF INDIA

Many Indian people came here on work visas. These are for people with special skills. **Engineering** is one example.

Many doctors and computer programmers get work visas, too. Work visas allow people to live and work here. They can live here even if they are not yet **citizens**.

Immigrating is harder for those without a good education. It is also harder if they don't have family members here.

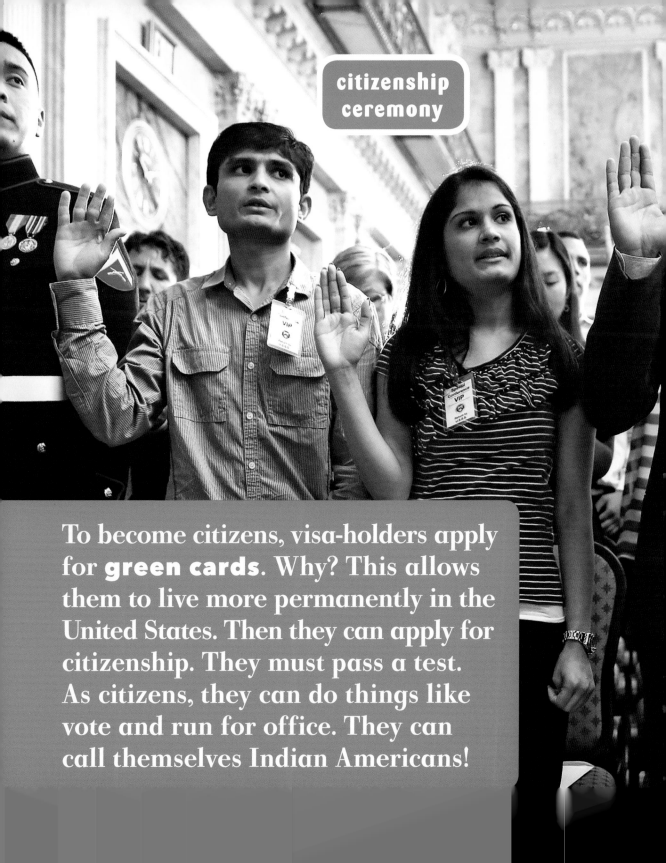

citizenship ceremony

To become citizens, visa-holders apply for **green cards**. Why? This allows them to live more permanently in the United States. Then they can apply for citizenship. They must pass a test. As citizens, they can do things like vote and run for office. They can call themselves Indian Americans!

TAKE A LOOK!

· ·

Indian immigrants live across the United States. What states had the most Indian immigrants living in them between 2013 and 2017? Take a look at these **estimates**!

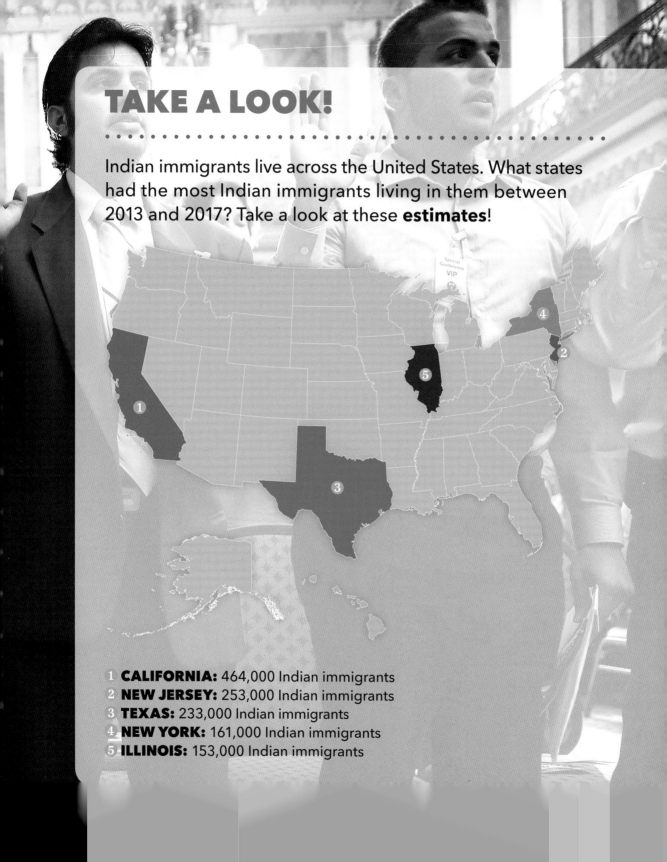

1 **CALIFORNIA:** 464,000 Indian immigrants
2 **NEW JERSEY:** 253,000 Indian immigrants
3 **TEXAS:** 233,000 Indian immigrants
4 **NEW YORK:** 161,000 Indian immigrants
5 **ILLINOIS:** 153,000 Indian immigrants

CHAPTER 3

A NEW HOME

Indian immigrants have many new experiences. Parts of the country are cold. They may need winter coats for the first time. They might need to learn to drive. Kids go to new schools.

They might miss family in India. They might not find their favorite foods in the grocery store. Sometimes, they face **prejudice**. People might have trouble saying their names.

Holi

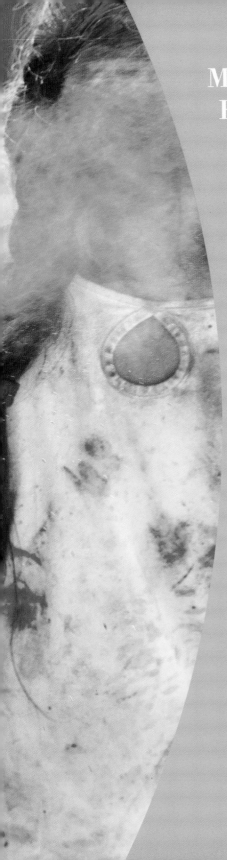

Many celebrate Indian holidays! Holi is one. It is the Hindu Festival of Colors. It is in spring. It celebrates the wheat **harvest**. People throw colored powder and water on one another. They listen to music, dance, and eat sweet treats.

LEARN THE CULTURE!

Eid al-Fitr is an important Indian holiday. Muslims celebrate it. It is the end of a month-long **fast**. They have a feast.

Many Indian Americans run businesses. They run for political office. They play professional sports.

Indian Americans are our friends and neighbors! We all call America home.

LEARN THE CULTURE!

Many Indians in America cook Indian food. Like what? They often eat vegetable or meat **curries**. They might drink **chai**. The food they make may change based on where they are from.

QUICK FACTS & TOOLS

AT A GLANCE

AFGHANISTAN

Himalayas

CHINA

PAKISTAN

BHUTAN

★ New Delhi

NEPAL

MYANMAR

INDIA

BANGLADESH

Arabian Sea

Indian Ocean

SRI LANKA

N
W — E
S

Number of Indian people living in other countries as of 2017: 16.6 million

Number of U.S. work visas for special skills issued to Indian immigrants in 2016: about 255,300

Number of Indian immigrants who became U.S. citizens in 2017: 50,802

Most common U.S. states for relocation: California, New Jersey, Texas, New York, Illinois

Most common languages spoken by Indian immigrants: English, Hindi, Telugu, Gujarati, Tamil, Punjabi

GLOSSARY

chai: A type of tea made with milk, sugar, and cardamom.

citizens: People who have full rights in a certain country, such as the right to work and the right to vote.

climate: The weather typical of a certain place over a long period of time.

crops: Plants grown for food.

curries: Dishes cooked in a spiced sauce, often served with rice.

engineering: A set of skills that uses math and science to solve society's problems and create things that humans use.

estimates: Rough or approximate numbers.

fast: A time during which people refrain from eating or eating particular foods.

green cards: Permits, called Lawful Permanent Resident Cards, that allow immigrants and refugees to live in the United States permanently.

harvest: The gathering of crops that are ready to eat.

immigrate: To leave one country to settle permanently in another.

prejudice: An opinion that is formed about a person or a group of people before getting to know them.

temples: Buildings used for worship.

visas: Stamps on a passport that say a person can come into a country for a certain period of time. There are different types of visas depending on the reasons people may want to visit or live in a different country.

INDEX

TO LEARN MORE

Finding more information is as easy as 1, 2, 3.

1. Go to www.factsurfer.com
2. Enter "Indian-Americanjourney" into the search box.
3. Choose your cover to see a list of websites.

FACT SURFER